Original title:
The Secret World

Copyright © 2024 Creative Arts Management OÜ
All rights reserved.

Author: Nash Everly
ISBN HARDBACK: 978-9916-88-886-5
ISBN PAPERBACK: 978-9916-88-887-2

Echoes of the Unspoken

Silent whispers drift through night,
Echoes linger, taking flight.
Words unsaid, feelings confined,
In shadows deep, love intertwined.

Footsteps falter on hidden paths,
Moments swallowed, lost in laughs.
Voices fade but hearts remain,
In the void, a haunting pain.

Chambers of Wonder

Within the walls of dreams we dwell,
Wonders wrapped in magic's spell.
Light beams dance on ancient stone,
In every corner, stories grown.

Whispers of truths, secrets unfold,
In chambers where the brave and bold.
Journey through realms both near and far,
Guided by a distant star.

Dimensional Façades

Layers peel like pages torn,
Truths unveiled, realities worn.
Masks we wear, faces collide,
In mirrored dreams, we seek to hide.

Fleeting visions of what could be,
In the fabric of mystery.
Dimensions shift with every thought,
In this space, we are caught.

The Uncharted Spectrum

Beyond the colors we have known,
An uncharted spectrum, yet to be shown.
Vibrant hues that bend and sway,
In twilight's glow, they softly play.

Binary thoughts in a world so wide,
Emotions flare, yet often hide.
In this dance of light and dark,
We find the fire, the hidden spark.

Ethereal Paths

Underneath the twilight skies,
Whispers dance on gentle winds,
Footsteps trace the fading light,
Where the spirit's journey begins.

Shadows flit through silver trees,
Secrets held by ancient ground,
Moonlit paths of mystery,
In silence, the heart is found.

The Lantern's Secret

A lantern glows in the still night,
Casting warmth on dreams that roam,
It holds the tales of lost delight,
A guiding star, a distant home.

Each flicker speaks of joy and pain,
Of journeys shut, and loves that grew,
In its light, hope we contain,
The secret paths we never flew.

The Hidden Odyssey

Beneath the waves of time and tide,
Lies a tale both deep and wide,
In every heart, a map awaits,
To seek the truth beyond the gates.

Footsteps echo on the shore,
Waves that whisper, hushing lore,
With every step, new worlds unfold,
In hidden journeys, dreams are told.

Mirage of Existence

In the desert of our thoughts,
Mirages flicker, dance, and sway,
What is real, what merely twirls,
In the heat of the briefest day?

Waves of sand blur past our feet,
Illusions invite, shadows play,
Yet within the heart's deep beat,
Truth awaits, a soft ballet.

Gossamer Crossroads

In the hush of dawn's embrace,
Whispers dance on the cool breeze,
Paths twist beneath silver lace,
Time flows like the swaying trees.

Beneath the skies of azure hue,
Footsteps tread on silken ground,
Choices linger, both old and new,
In the silence, echoes resound.

Each turn a world to explore,
Where shadows mingle with the light,
Gossamer threads, forevermore,
Guide the wanderers through the night.

In dreams, the crossroads come alive,
The heart makes its final choice,
Through every doubt, we learn to thrive,
In unity, we find our voice.

Enchanted Footsteps

Through the forest, soft and deep,
Footsteps weave a vibrant tale,
With every step, secrets keep,
From the brook to the grassy vale.

Moonlight dapples on the ground,
Whispers of a magic near,
In the night, the lost are found,
Guided by the starlit sphere.

Mushrooms glow in twilight's hand,
Each path a promise, wild and free,
A symphony of nature's band,
Calls to hearts in harmony.

Here, the world turns slow and bright,
Every shadow tells its truth,
With enchanted dreams in sight,
We dance again, embracing youth.

The Obscured Sanctuary

Hidden deep from prying eyes,
Where the forgotten stories rest,
Beneath the ancient, sprawling skies,
Lies a place where souls are blessed.

With ivy draped on crumbling stone,
And laughter kissed by silent air,
Time feels different, yet unknown,
In this refuge, free from care.

The whispers of the willow trees,
Speak of love and of our fears,
In every rustle, memories,
Flow like water through the years.

Lost within this sacred space,
Hearts unify in tender grace,
In the obscured sanctuary,
Life's tapestry finds its place.

Voices of the Unseen

In shadows deep, where silence dwells,
A symphony of whispers rise,
The hidden tales, like secret spells,
Are woven through the moonlit skies.

With every heartbeat, stories swell,
In distant dreams, we catch their sound,
They speak of love, of time they fell,
From lips of stars, their truths unbound.

Listen close, the night will sing,
Of journeys taken and the lost,
In every echo, memories cling,
Glimmers of what we yearn, and cost.

Voices beckon from afar,
In gentle tones, they guide our way,
With spirits bright, like flick'ring stars,
They light our path, night turns to day.

The Invisible Thread

In shadows where whispers softly tread,
Fates entwined by a filament thread.
Hearts connected, yet worlds apart,
Silent connections, the language of heart.

Mysteries dance in the twilight's glow,
Binding souls in a tapestry slow.
Through the distance, love finds its way,
In the silence, it yearns to stay.

Haunting Facades

Behind the smiles, a story concealed,
Burdened souls that refuse to yield.
Masks worn heavy, a poignant guise,
Hiding dreams 'neath the watchful skies.

Echoes linger in the hollow night,
Yearning for warmth, seeking the light.
But in the shadows, the truth unravels,
A haunting tale where beauty travels.

The Cloaked Symphony

Notes collide in a ghostly embrace,
Whispers of music fill empty space.
Strings of fate pull at the heart,
Each melody, a work of art.

In the silence, a rhythm brews,
A cloaked symphony of vibrant hues.
When night falls, the melody plays,
Unlocking dreams in mysterious ways.

Unveiling the Unseen

Beneath the surface, the layers unfold,
Stories of lives in whispers told.
With every glance, a world emerges,
In the quiet, reality converges.

Veils of doubt slowly cast aside,
The unseen truths we cannot hide.
With open hearts, we dare to see,
The beauty that lies in the mystery.

Lurking in Plain Sight

In the shadow of the day,
Whispers weave through the air,
Secrets dance on the wind,
Cloaked in the mundane stare.

Faces pass, eyes unseeing,
Echoes of what was lost,
Dancing in the twilight,
A ghostly warmth embossed.

Silent stories unfold,
In corners where we tread,
A tapestry of hidden
Where only silence led.

Look again, there's magic,
In the threads of routine,
For all that's truly alive,
Lurks just out of our glean.

The Enchanted Threshold

Beneath the arching boughs,
Lies a path of mystery,
A threshold to wonders,
Where dreams weave their history.

Leaves shimmer with secrets,
In hues of twilight dreams,
As whispers of old tales
Flow softly like moonbeams.

With each step, a heartbeat,
Time folds and interweaves,
Through gardens of the lost,
Where the mind believes.

Cross gently to the other,
Where magic stirs the night,
For every stone and shadow
Holds an enchanted light.

Hidden Currents

Beneath the surface flowing,
Lies a river, dark and deep,
Currents whisper secrets,
In waters calm, they seep.

Roots entangled, stories,
In silence, they entwine,
What lies beneath the surface
Wants to break from the line.

Eyes unseen in reflections,
Glimmers of what has been,
Lurking in every shadow,
Tales of hope unforeseen.

Catch the echoes of the past,
In drops of fleeting rain,
For hidden currents linger,
Where the heart knows its chain.

Phantasmal Journeys

In dreams, we chase the shadows,
Through corridors of light,
Wandering through the echoes,
Of time's eternal night.

Each step a fleeting whisper,
A dance with fate's own hand,
Skimming through the pages,
Of a soft, mysterious land.

Phantom roads stretch before us,
Marking paths yet untried,
Spirits twirl in the twilight,
Bearing secrets inside.

Embrace the phantasmal calling,
Where horizons gently sway,
For every journey beckons,
To chase the dawn's first ray.

Labyrinths of the Mind

In corridors of thought we tread,
Lost in echoes of what we've said.
Shadows dance on flickering walls,
Whispers rise as reason falls.

Paths diverge in tangled dreams,
Fractured truths reveal their seams.
Riddles cloaked in silent schemes,
Each answer bursts with silent screams.

A spiral winding ever deep,
Memories we sow, we reap.
Drifting through this maze of time,
Awakened thoughts begin to rhyme.

Yet amid the winding strife,
We search for meaning, seek for life.
In labyrinths the brave may find,
A glimpse of peace within the mind.

Secrets in the Breeze

Gentle whispers ride the air,
Secrets linger everywhere.
Leaves confide in softest tones,
Nature sings to hearts alone.

The rustling grass, a lover's sigh,
Memories carried as they fly.
Fragrance dances, time stands still,
In the hush, we feel the thrill.

Clouds unravel old distress,
In their shadows, we find rest.
Each gust breathes out a hidden truth,
Life unfolds, restoring youth.

Listen closely, let it tease,
Stories told by wandering trees.
In every breeze, a tale unfolds,
A sacred bond, the world beholds.

The Other Side of the Veil

Beneath the surface, worlds collide,
Beyond the veil lies what we hide.
Veiled in shadows, light will peek,
Whispers linger, silence speaks.

Time stands still in veils of dreams,
Where nothing's ever as it seems.
Reality bends, truth sways,
In twilight's grasp, the spirit plays.

Glimmers of hope in the unknown,
Heartfelt messages, seeds are sown.
Curiosity pulls us near,
To the other side, we feel no fear.

In soft reflections, we unite,
Bridging realms into the light.
With every breath, we dare to sail,
Towards the mystery beyond the veil.

Fragments of a Hidden Life

In shadows cast by morning light,
Fragments of dreams take flight.
Pieces lost, yet somehow whole,
Hidden depths within the soul.

Moments flicker like a flame,
Whispers echo, yet the same.
Scattered thoughts across the floor,
Unlocking memories once more.

Through winding paths of silent grace,
We chase reflections, find our place.
Each fragment tells a story true,
Of lives unlived and skies so blue.

In every shard, a truth reveals,
A tapestry that time conceals.
Hidden lives, a dance, a strife,
In the fragments, we find life.

Unfolding Dreams

In the silence of the night,
Whispers float like feathered light.
Stars awaken with a sigh,
Painting visions in the sky.

Dancing shadows drift and glide,
Each one holds a secret wide.
Time unravels, moments gleam,
Life transforms within a dream.

Softly echoes of the past,
Moments gone, but shadows cast.
Every heartbeat, every glance,
Leads us deeper in this dance.

Awake or lost, who can tell?
In this dreamscape, we all dwell.
Threads of hope, fears interlace,
In unfolding dreams, we find grace.

The Labyrinth of Lore

In ancient halls where echoes play,
Stories linger, night turns to day.
Each corner holds a tale unknown,
Paths converge, yet we're all alone.

Faded tomes and whispered rhymes,
Chronicles of forgotten times.
Hidden clues in every seam,
The labyrinth calls, it's more than a dream.

With each step, the shadows sway,
Guiding us along the way.
Forked roads and twisted fates,
What lies beyond these heavy gates?

The heart races, a path unwinds,
A journey where truth entwines.
Endless questions, woven lore,
In the dim light, we thirst for more.

The Surreal Bazaar

Through vibrant stalls with colors bright,
A world awakens in soft twilight.
Dreamlike wares adorn each space,
Mysteries woven with gentle grace.

Silken threads and fragrant spice,
Curiosities that entice.
Glimmers of stories in each craft,
The mundane and magic softly graft.

Figures dance in laughter's glow,
Visitors lost, nowhere to go.
Bartering dreams with moments rare,
In the bazaar, hearts lay bare.

Amidst the chaos, time stands still,
Each item whispers, beckons, fills.
A labyrinth of sights unseen,
In the surreal, we find our sheen.

Flickers of the Unseen

In shadows cast by fading light,
Whispers flutter, taking flight.
Echoes of thoughts we dare not speak,
Flickers of dreams, both strong and weak.

Through twilight's veil, visions spark,
Illuminating paths once dark.
In quiet moments, truths unfold,
The unseen glimmers, brave and bold.

Eyes wide open to the night,
Searching for what feels so right.
Every flicker tells a tale,
A gentle breeze, a thrilling gale.

In the silence, we embrace,
The hidden world, a sacred space.
Forever drawn to that soft gleam,
In the flickers, we find our dream.

Beneath the Surface

In shadows deep, a whisper flows,
Where secrets dance in undertows.
Glimmers hide in depths unclear,
A world unknown, we draw near.

Silent currents, tales they weave,
Of lost desires and dreams we grieve.
With every pulse, the waters sing,
Of hidden truths that arise in spring.

Beneath the waves, the stories wait,
As tides of time drift past the gate.
The heart of oceans beats so bold,
Revealing wonders, yet untold.

So dive within, embrace the flow,
Explore the depths of all we know.
For in the dark, beauty spins,
Beneath the surface, new life begins.

Enigmas of Twilight

In twilight's glow, the shadows stir,
Whispers lost in a gentle blur.
Colors blend, a mystic trance,
Where secrets hide in a fleeting dance.

The stars awaken, one by one,
As day fades out, the night is spun.
A tapestry woven, night and light,
In the soft embrace of coming night.

Silhouetted forms take flight on air,
Enigmas breathe without a care.
In the hush, the world transforms,
A symphony of calming norms.

What truth is held within the dusk?
In every shadow, every husk.
For in the quiet, mysteries bloom,
Enigmas of twilight dispel the gloom.

Dreamscapes Unveiled

Beyond the veil where dreamers tread,
A land of visions, softly spread.
The air hums sweet with hopes and fears,
As night unveils what day concears.

Mountains rise from thoughts untold,
While rivers weave through past and gold.
In this realm, the heart finds wings,
And freedom sings of boundless things.

A kaleidoscope of fleeting sights,
Where time is lost in endless flights.
With every breath, a journey starts,
In dreamscapes that will touch our hearts.

Awake, we seek what's hidden deep,
Yet dreams remind us of what we keep.
For in the night, the spirit soars,
Unveiling depths with cosmic doors.

Paths of the Unseen

In quiet corners, whispers fade,
Paths unwind in a mystic braid.
Each step a choice, a chance to roam,
Through shadows thick to find a home.

The winding trails, both sharp and smooth,
Reveal the secrets they can soothe.
With every footfall, stories blend,
On paths of the unseen, we transcend.

Ghostly echoes guide the way,
In twilight's glow, where dreams can sway.
Each turn unveils a hidden gate,
Leading to fates we contemplate.

So take the road less traveled by,
Beneath the wide and starry sky.
For in the journey, life will gleam,
On paths of the unseen, we dream.

Mystique in the Mist

Veils of fog hold whispered dreams,
Softly drifting, silent streams.
Moonlight dances, spirits sigh,
Secrets linger, nights pass by.

Footsteps echo on damp ground,
Hidden wonders all around.
Shadows twirl, enchantment wakes,
In the mist, the magic stakes.

A haunting melody flows near,
Calling forth what we hold dear.
Lost in time, we find our way,
Mystique charms the break of day.

In the twilight, stillness grows,
Within the mist, our longing glows.
Caught between the worlds we roam,
In this shroud, we find our home.

Elysian Shadows

Underneath the silent trees,
Elysium breathes with gentle ease.
Shadows dance on emerald blades,
Whispers weave through leafy glades.

Softly painted sunlight streams,
Awakening the heart's bright dreams.
Here the soul finds refuge warm,
Sheltered from the world's harsh storm.

In this realm of vibrant hues,
Nature's melody we choose.
Lost in rapture, spirits soar,
In the shadows, we explore.

Let tranquility unfold,
In this haven, stories told.
Elysian whispers softly call,
In their embrace, we feel it all.

Beneath the Echoing Canopy

Roots entwined in ancient ground,
Echoes of the past resound.
Through the branches, life cascades,
Underneath the green parades.

Rustling leaves, a gentle sway,
Nature sings in sweet ballet.
Light filters down, a golden beam,
Promising the sweetest dream.

All the creatures stir and play,
Under canopy, night and day.
Here in quiet, peace abides,
Where the earth and spirit slides.

Beneath the echoes, hearts unite,
Within the woods, pure delight.
In the stillness, we lose track,
In this haven, no turning back.

Journey into the Obscure

Paths unmarked by time's cruel hand,
Footprints lead to whispered land.
Eyes wide open, secrets blend,
On this journey, rules may bend.

Into shadows, dreams take flight,
Unraveling the veil of night.
Stars above a guiding light,
In the dark, we find our sight.

Every turn a story spun,
Fading echoes, now begun.
Lost in wonder, we embrace,
The obscurity's warm embrace.

Endless roads where visions sway,
With each step, we drift away.
In the depths, our spirit stirs,
Journey's end, where magic whirs.

Obscured Horizons

The sun dips low in the haze,
Shadows stretch in twilight's gaze.
Waves of light dance on the ground,
Silent whispers all around.

Clouds conceal the distant shore,
Mysteries behind the door.
Footsteps trace forgotten paths,
Echoes linger, nature laughs.

Colors blend in twilight's blend,
Yet the day begins to end.
Stars awaken, softly bright,
Guiding dreams into the night.

Hopes once clear, now twist and turn,
In the dark, our spirits burn.
Finding peace in what we seek,
Among the shadows, we are meek.

Veiled Encounters

Beneath the gaze of silver moons,
Lies a world that softly croons.
Timid hearts take careful steps,
In the silence, love adept.

Whispers float like autumn leaves,
Secrets held beneath the eaves.
Eyes that spark with veiled intent,
Moments shared, no words are spent.

Fingers brush and stories weave,
In the night, they dare believe.
Chance encounters in a dream,
Life's a gentle, fleeting stream.

Through the mist, they find the light,
In the dark, they hold on tight.
Veils may hide, but hearts unveil,
Love's soft touch will always trail.

The Silence of Dreams

In the hush where shadows play,
Dreams arise at close of day.
Thoughts like butterflies take flight,
In the stillness of the night.

Minds entwined in quiet grace,
Images begin to trace.
Whispers echo, soft and clear,
In the silence, hope draws near.

Stars above ignite the vast,
Each a wish from ages past.
In the dark, the mind's a stream,
Flowing freely through each dream.

Awake or sleep, it's hard to tell,
In this place where spirits dwell.
Moments linger, time stands still,
In the silence, hearts fulfill.

Secrets of the Twilight Grove

In the grove where shadows loom,
Whispers hide amidst the gloom.
Branches sway with tales untold,
Secrets flourish, bright and bold.

Moonlight filters through the leaves,
Nature's heart, it gently breathes.
Every rustle, every sigh,
Holds the truth we can't deny.

Footfalls soft on ancient ground,
Echoes of the past resound.
Time stands still in this embrace,
In the grove, we share a space.

Mysteries wrapped in twilight's shroud,
Underneath the watching cloud.
Come and see what nature knows,
In the heart of twilight's prose.

Celestial Oddities

Stars dance above in silent glee,
Nebulas swirl in cosmic spree.
Planets hum their ancient song,
In the vastness, we all belong.

Comets trail with fiery grace,
Touching lives in boundless space.
In the night, dreams take flight,
Guided by celestial light.

Galaxies twist in the dark,
Whispering secrets, leaving a mark.
Each twinkle holds a tale untold,
In the universe, brave and bold.

So look up high, let your spirit soar,
For in the sky, there's always more.
The oddities we seek and find,
Are reflections of the curious mind.

Gossamer Threads

Delicate strands in morning dew,
Weaving whispers, soft and true.
Nature's lace, with colors bright,
Catch the dawn's first golden light.

Through the trees, the breezes sigh,
Gossamer threads that flutter by.
Each moment glimmers, a fleeting grace,
In the quiet, we find our place.

Spiders spin with patient skill,
Tales of wonder, hearts to fill.
In the tapestry of the day,
Life unfolds in gentle sway.

So cherish each fragile dream,
For life is more than it may seem.
In delicate forms, we're intertwined,
By gossamer threads, we are aligned.

Abandoned Sanctuaries

Whispers echo in silent halls,
Where ivy climbs and shadows fall.
Once filled with laughter, joy and tears,
Now haunted by the passing years.

The windows gaze with dusty eyes,
Facing the world, under somber skies.
Memories linger in every nook,
Stories trapped in an old, worn book.

Nature reclaims what man lets go,
With wildflowers in soft, vibrant glow.
In solitude, the heart can mend,
Finding beauty in what transcends.

So wander through these sacred ruins,
Where time stands still, and peace is brewing.
In the abandoned, solace awaits,
In forgotten paths, we navigate.

Illuminated Whispers

In candlelight, soft voices blend,
Secrets shared with a gentle bend.
Shadows dance upon the wall,
Stories whispered, inviting all.

Moonlight kisses the silent night,
Bathing the world in silver light.
Each breath carries an ancient lore,
A tapestry woven, forevermore.

In the stillness, hearts open wide,
To the whispers that softly glide.
In the darkness, we find our dreams,
Illuminated by gentle beams.

So listen close, let the silence speak,
In luminous moments, we find the meek.
For in every whisper, there lies a spark,
Guiding us through the shadowed dark.

Hidden Realms

In the forest deep and wide,
Where the secrets often hide,
Whispers ride on breezes light,
Guiding wanderers through the night.

Beneath the roots and leaves aglow,
Mysteries begin to flow,
A dance of shadows, soft and sleek,
In hidden realms, the lost do seek.

Ancient echoes softly call,
In enchanted groves, we fall,
To worlds where time and space entwine,
In the solace where stars align.

Through the mist, a pathway gleams,
Luring hearts with woven dreams,
In these realms where magic sways,
A sanctuary where hope stays.

Whispers in the Shadows

In the corners of the night,
Where secrets shun the light,
Whispers float like whispers low,
In hidden crevices, they flow.

Silhouettes behind the trees,
Carried gently by the breeze,
Voices soft, a haunting sound,
In the depths where lost are found.

Echoes calling from the dark,
Soft as dying daylight's spark,
Step by step, the heartbeats race,
As shadows weave a silent space.

Through the veil of softest gloom,
Whispers twine like flowers bloom,
In this dance of dark and bright,
We unveil the hidden light.

Veils of Enchantment

In the twilight's soft embrace,
Magic dances, leaves a trace,
Veils of mist in soft descent,
Hold the whispers of content.

Glimmers twinkle in the air,
Threads of dreams both bright and rare,
Through the dusk, our spirits soar,
Chasing tales from ancient lore.

Each petal falls, a wish released,
In the silence, hearts are teased,
Veils of enchantment softly spin,
A tapestry where dreams begin.

Beneath the stars, the night unfolds,
Stories whispered, secrets told,
In the glow of moonlit streams,
Veils of enchantment weave our dreams.

Echoes of the Unknown

In the caverns deep and vast,
Whispers of the future past,
Echoes bounce on stony walls,
Where the stillness gently calls.

Footsteps tracing paths unseen,
Through the shadows, lights may glean,
Every echo holds a tale,
In the void, our thoughts set sail.

Time a river, flowing free,
Carrying the lost decree,
Beneath the darkened skies we roam,
To find what leads us back to home.

In the silence, we may find,
Echoes of a distant mind,
Tracing back through realms we've grown,
To the essence of the unknown.

Chronicles of the Concealed

In shadows cast by whispered tales,
Secrets linger where light pales.
Beneath the surface, truths reside,
Hidden gems where dreams abide.

Silent echoes in the night,
Flicker softly, faintly bright.
A journey veiled in mystic lore,
Calling hearts to seek once more.

Through narrow paths and winding turns,
The flame of knowledge ever burns.
Unraveled tales, a gift undone,
Beneath the moon, the past is spun.

In the quiet, secrets bloom,
Filling every shadowed room.
Chronicles that time has penned,
In the dark, we find a friend.

Tides of Mystery

Waves that crash upon the shore,
Whispers from the ocean's core.
Salty winds carry the past,
Secrets tethered, deep and vast.

Underneath the starlit sky,
Questions rise, like seabirds fly.
Each tide brings a tale anew,
An endless quest for what is true.

In every ebb, in every flow,
The unknown beckons us to go.
Footprints washed away in sand,
Yet memories make their stand.

A horizon shrouded in mist,
What's unseen can still exist.
As we sail through dreams untold,
The tides of mystery unfold.

Threads of Illusion

In a fabric woven tight,
Colors warping in the light.
Patterns shift and dance away,
Truths concealed in soft array.

Threads that tangle, twist and bind,
Reality's a fickle kind.
What we see may not be real,
The heart's desire is to feel.

Layers deep, illusions weave,
A tapestry we can't perceive.
With every stitch, the vision grows,
Fleeting glimpses of what we know.

In every corner, shadows play,
Chasing light, they fade away.
Yet in the dusk, beauty lies,
In woven dreams and painted skies.

Gardens of the Unspoken

In silence thrives a secret grove,
Where whispers bloom, and time can rove.
Petals soft with unshared dreams,
Beneath the boughs, the spirit beams.

A gentle touch, a hidden glance,
In stillness grows a quiet dance.
Roots entwined in harmony,
Nurtured by the mystery.

Every shade a story veils,
In the breeze, the heart inhales.
Among the leaves, the tales unfold,
A garden rich with truths untold.

Where silence speaks, and fears take flight,
The unspoken finds its light.
In this refuge, souls unite,
In gardens blooming, dreams take flight.

Forgotten Pathways

In shadows deep, where echoes sigh,
Old trails linger, where whispers lie.
Leaves dance softly, memories greet,
Each step taken, a story complete.

Moonlight glimmers on stones so worn,
Footprints fading, souls reborn.
Through tangled thickets, secrets blend,
Time's gentle kindness, a faithful friend.

The air holds tales of those who passed,
Unseen moments, forever cast.
Branches cradle their silent woes,
As nature weaves the life it chose.

Forgotten pathways call to roam,
In nature's heart, we find our home.
With every turn, a new refrain,
And in the journey, loss and gain.

Tales from the Underbrush

Beneath the ferns, where shadows rest,
Life unfolds in a hidden nest.
Whispers flutter on the air,
Each rustle speaks of tales laid bare.

The trail is marked by tiny paws,
And chirps of creatures without pause.
Bright-eyed hedgehogs cross the lane,
While crickets strum a twilight refrain.

In tangled roots, old stories lie,
Of fleeting dreams that float on by.
A world alive in colors bright,
Emerging softly from the night.

Tales from the underbrush are spun,
In ecosystem's dance, we're all one.
So listen closely, hear the song,
For in this world, we all belong.

Spectral Gardens

In spectral gardens, shadows play,
Where flowers bloom in shades of gray.
Petals whisper ancient lore,
And beckon souls to wander more.

Ghostly winds weave through the trees,
Carrying secrets on the breeze.
Each blossom holds a spirit's dream,
Awakening life in soft moonbeam.

Glimmers of light among the leaves,
A tapestry that softly weaves.
The night reveals what day conceals,
In every heart, a longing heals.

In spectral gardens, we may find,
The echoes of a restless mind.
With gentle care, we seek to learn,
The beauty in the shades that turn.

Mysteries in Twilight

As daylight fades, the mysteries rise,
Beneath the cloak of amber skies.
The stars awaken, tales undone,
In twilight's grasp, the night is spun.

Shapes begin to blur and blend,
And with the dusk, old moments mend.
Each shadow dances, a fleeting chance,
To glimpse the secrets in their trance.

The moon ascends with silver grace,
Illuminating the hidden space.
Where dreams and reality intertwine,
In this quiet hour, all is divine.

Mysteries in twilight softly call,
Inviting hearts to rise and fall.
In every heartbeat, magic swells,
In whispered tales, the spirit dwells.

Hidden Realms

Beyond the veil, where shadows creep,
Whispers of secrets, in silence keep.
In the twilight, where dreams unfold,
A world of magic, quietly told.

Within the forest, paths entwine,
Glimmers of starlight, pure and fine.
Echoes of laughter, lost in the trees,
The heart beats softly, a gentle breeze.

Through hidden gates, the past reveals,
Stories of old, in spiraled reels.
Ancient echoes, in the mist of night,
Calling the wanderers, guiding their flight.

In every shadow, a tale resides,
Life intertwined, where time abides.
With every step, the mysteries bloom,
In hidden realms, where the spirits loom.

Enigmatic Echoes

In the silence, a voice will rise,
Carried on winds, beneath dark skies.
Each word a ripple, across the pond,
Lost in the moment, but forever fond.

Whispers of wisdom, trapped in the air,
A dance of shadows, flickering there.
The mind's reflection, a fleeting glance,
Caught in the echoes, lost in the trance.

Time bends softly, revealing the past,
In enigmatic echoes, memories cast.
Forgotten stories seek to unfold,
With each soft murmur, legends retold.

In the twilight, where secrets blend,
A tapestry woven, without an end.
Embrace the echoes, let them entwine,
For in their whispers, true hearts align.

Surreal Sanctuaries

In landscapes painted with dreams and light,
A sanctuary blooms, out of sight.
Clouds of illusion drift like mist,
In these realms, reality twists.

Fleeting moments, suspended in grace,
Time takes a backseat in this sacred space.
Colors collide in a dazzling dance,
Lost in the rhythm, we take a chance.

Each breath a canvas, each heartbeat a song,
In surreal sanctuaries, we belong.
A mirror reflecting the soul's deep needs,
Where every thought plants vibrant seeds.

Amongst the wonders, we find our way,
In softest whispers, night meets day.
A haven of dreams, where hearts can soar,
In these surreal sanctuaries, forevermore.

Veils of Mystery

Beneath the surface, a world concealed,
Veils of mystery, gently unsealed.
With every glance, the unknown calls,
Enticing the curious, as darkness falls.

Whispers linger in the quiet air,
Secrets woven with delicate care.
In shadowy corners, stories lie,
Waiting for seekers, to venture nigh.

Time holds its breath, a thief in the night,
In veils of mystery, shadows take flight.
Each step reveals a truth yet untold,
In the silence, adventures unfold.

Embrace the enigma, let it inspire,
In the heart's shadows, feel the fire.
For within the veils, life's wonders breathe,
Whispering softly, what we believe.

The Scribe of Shadows

In the dim light where whispers dwell,
A scribe writes tales that none can tell.
Ink of midnight, paper of dreams,
Captured in silence, lost in streams.

With every stroke, a secret unfolds,
Stories of bravery, fears untold.
He weaves the night with threads of gold,
In shadows' embrace, his heart is bold.

Each parchment sighs with ancient lore,
Tales of longing, and battles of yore.
In the quiet hours, his pen ignites,
A symphony woven in starry nights.

For every echo that time creates,
The scribe immortalizes our fates.
In shadows' dance, his legend grows,
A guardian of truths in twilight's throes.

Alchemy of Secrets

In the cauldron of night, potions brew,
Whispers of magic, a world anew.
Essences gathered from earth and sky,
Alchemy blooms as shadows fly.

A flicker of flame, a dash of spice,
Transforming the mundane, oh so nice.
Secrets unveiled in the bubbling mist,
Each drop a promise, a magic twist.

With careful hands, the alchemist toils,
Turning the mundane into precious foils.
Ciphers of wisdom, hidden in glass,
Lessons forgotten, now ready to pass.

In each potion lies a story untold,
Of a heart that's daring, of spirit bold.
Alchemy whispers in twilight's embrace,
A dance of secrets, a timeless grace.

Beneath the Surface

Beneath the waves, where silence reigns,
Secrets are held in watery veins.
Echoes of life in depths profound,
Lost to the surface, yet ever found.

Coral kingdoms and shadows play,
Mysteries hidden in gentle sway.
Fish weave tales in colors bright,
In the crystal depths, lost from sight.

Ancient whispers from the ocean floor,
Tell of the ages, of love and lore.
In the depth's embrace, stories align,
Time stands still, fate intertwines.

The world above fades, a distant song,
Beneath the surface, where souls belong.
In every ripple, a heart's refrain,
The ocean's embrace, both joy and pain.

Where Fantasies Roam

In a realm where dreams take flight,
Fantasies bloom in the soft twilight.
Castles gleam on clouds of cream,
Whispers of magic knit every seam.

Wandering paths, through starlit glades,
Adventures await in gentle shades.
Creatures of wonder, spirits of grace,
Dancing in shadows, a timeless space.

With every heartbeat, the story grows,
With vivid colors and radiant prose.
In laughter and song, the echoes flow,
Where hearts are light and love will sow.

Beyond the horizon, the fantasy glows,
In this sacred land where time slows.
Embrace the magic, let your heart soar,
In the realm of dreams, forevermore.

Liminal Spaces

In the shadow's edge we stand,
Where silence speaks, a gentle hand.
Footsteps fade on the worn-out stair,
Transitional moments linger in air.

A whisper of dreams begins to rise,
Beyond the veil where the unknown lies.
Fleeting glances, a fleeting chance,
In this twilight, we slowly dance.

Caught between night and break of dawn,
The world is still, the path less drawn.
Here we linger, caught in thought,
In ephemeral spaces, we're sought.

What lies ahead, what do we find?
In the liminal, we unwind.
The borders blur, reality bends,
In this threshold, our spirit mends.

Shrouded Tales

Beneath the fabric, secrets hide,
In shadows deep, where whispers bide.
Ancient stories, untold and worn,
In dusty tomes, from nights forlorn.

The flicker of lanterns casts their glow,
Revealing paths where few dare go.
Characters dwell in fleeted time,
In tangled plots, their fates entwined.

Through veils of mist, we wander slow,
Each twist revealing, a tale to sow.
In every corner, echoes dwell,
Of lost voices, and forgotten spells.

With every turn, a truth unveiled,
In shrouded tales, we are impaled.
To journey through, the past reclaims,
Our destinies spun in whispered names.

Mirage Kasbah

In the desert's heart, an allure calls,
A shimmering sight, as daylight falls.
Winds rustle softly, secrets breathe,
In the mirage, we dare to believe.

Starlit skies above so vast,
A kasbah emerges, a glimpse from the past.
Tapestries weave stories in dust,
Where time loses grip, in sand we trust.

Echoes of laughter, shadows in play,
The warmth of spices, fading away.
In fleeting moments, reality bends,
As we seek a truth that seldom ends.

Through the illusion, the spirit soars,
In mirage kasbah, we find open doors.
To lost horizons, we're destined to roam,
In transient beauty, we find our home.

The Hidden Cartographer

With compass in hand, he charts unknown,
Mapping the lands where few have flown.
In ink and stars, a journey drawn,
The hidden paths call out at dawn.

Between the lines, adventure waits,
In secret places, beyond the gates.
Every step a story unfolds,
In the heart of lands, ancient and bold.

Across the mountains, beneath the sea,
He dances with shadows, wild and free.
Each mark a legend, each path a guide,
In the world's embrace, his heart resides.

For in the hidden, the magic lies,
In every journey, beneath the skies.
The cartographer's art, a life embraced,
In maps uncharted, we find our place.

Subconscious Landscapes

In shadows deep, where echoes dwell,
Thoughts like rivers weave and swell.
A canvas draped in kaleidoscope hues,
Where visions dance and timelines fuse.

Through tangled woods, the mind takes flight,
Among the stars that grace the night.
Each step reveals a hidden thread,
Of dreams and fears, both silently bred.

Beneath the surface, whispers call,
In silent chambers, where shadows fall.
A secret map of what was known,
In every heartbeat, deeply sown.

As horizons blur, boundaries fade,
In timeless realms, our thoughts parade.
A landscape forged of hopes and sighs,
Where the heart's desires ever rise.

Whispers from Beyond

In twilight's grace, a soft refrain,
A melody that stirs the brain.
Letters inked in silver light,
From realms unseen, out of sight.

Through veils so thin, we dare to hear,
Silent echoes drawing near.
Voices from the past they bring,
In fragile tones, like murmuring.

A gentle hush within the air,
Promises woven with tender care.
Each secret shared, a fleeting spark,
Illuminating shadows dark.

What lies beyond, we cannot know,
Yet in our hearts, the whispers flow.
A bridge of faith, a path we'll roam,
For in this dance, we find our home.

Mirage of Dreams

Upon the sands, reflections gleam,
Fleeting visions, like a dream.
Gold and azure, a shimmered glance,
Invites the soul to twirl and dance.

A world reborn in the mind's embrace,
Where hopes convert to time and space.
Through colorful prisms, wish upon stars,
In the ephemeral glow of fate's memoirs.

Caught in the web of what could be,
A fantasy spun, wild and free.
Each breath a wish, each sigh a scheme,
Floating softly on the stream.

Yet reality waits, with open arms,
To ground our hearts, unfold its charms.
In mirage's fade, the truth shall gleam,
For life awakens beyond the dream.

The Woven Unknown

In threads of fate, a tapestry lies,
Infinite patterns, under the skies.
Each stitch a tale, both bold and shy,
In the loom of time, where shadows sigh.

Interlaced moments, hearts that beat,
With secrets whispered, bittersweet.
A fabric dyed in love and strife,
Every color tells of life.

In corners hidden, stories hide,
Yearnings woven deep inside.
Mysterious knots that bind us tight,
In every tear, there shines a light.

Unravel the questions, embrace the quest,
For within the unknown, we find our rest.
In every thread, a world unfolds,
Where the heart's unspoken dreams are told.

Strings of the Ethereal

In whispers soft, the night unfolds,
A tapestry of silver and gold.
Stars dance above in gentle glee,
A melody that sets the heart free.

Beneath the moon, shadows play,
Illuminating dreams that sway.
The air is thick with secrets bright,
Carried softly on wings of light.

A symphony of distant calls,
The echoes of forgotten halls.
Each note a thread, a path to weave,
Into the soul, where we believe.

In the stillness, silence sings,
Awakening the hidden things.
With every breath, the world transforms,
As cosmic symphonies take their forms.

In the Thicket of Dreams

In the thicket, shadows creep,
Where silken wishes weave and leap.
A canopy of emerald green,
Hides the wonders yet unseen.

With every step, the air is deep,
Carrying secrets we long to keep.
Faint laughter lingers on the breeze,
A world enchanted, meant to please.

Through tangled vines, our thoughts do drift,
In this realm, all sorrows lift.
The heart finds solace, peace, and rest,
In dreams and fantasies, we are blessed.

As daylight fades, the magic swells,
In the thicket, where silence dwells.
A dance of shadows, a play of light,
In the realm of dreams, all feels right.

Riddles in the Quiet

In the quiet, riddles stir,
Murmurs soft like a gentle purr.
Questions hang in the empty air,
Whispers of truths that we can share.

A flicker here, a shadow there,
Hints of puzzles that dare to care.
In stillness, thoughts begin to bloom,
Filling the spaces of the room.

Answers twirl like autumn leaves,
Bound by fate or what one believes.
Every pause a doorway wide,
To the mysteries that bide inside.

In the hush, a heartbeat's grace,
In every silence, a hidden place.
Riddles linger, waiting to be found,
In quiet corners, wisdom abounds.

Forbidden Glades

In hidden glades, where shadows fall,
Secrets whispered, a timeless call.
Ancient trees with stories old,
Guard the truths that must be told.

With every step, the world does change,
Mysteries bloom, both dark and strange.
A twilight dance, a fervent chase,
In the forbidden, find our place.

The air is thick with longing sighs,
Phantom echoes and lost goodbyes.
A realm where dreams and fears collide,
In the glades, where spirits guide.

Through weeping willows, shadows twist,
Each moment fleeting, a fleeting mist.
In forbidden light, we dare to roam,
In nature's heart, we find our home.

Echoes Beneath the Surface

Beneath the waves, whispers dance,
Secrets held in water's trance.
Sediments of time, they swirl,
Lost reflections start to unfurl.

Rippling tales of ancient lore,
Shadows pulse on ocean's floor.
Echoes linger, soft and deep,
Memories in silence keep.

Coral castles, riddles weave,
In this realm, what do we believe?
Voices fade, yet still they sing,
Underneath, the past takes wing.

Diving down, the stillness grows,
Beneath the currents, wisdom flows.
Each heartbeat tells a story grand,
In the depths, we understand.

Portals of Imagination

Close your eyes and take a flight,
Into worlds defined by light.
Every dream a vibrant hue,
Painting visions fresh and new.

Through arches framed in wonder's grace,
Adventures wait in timeless space.
Thoughts can soar like birds in gleam,
Unbound by reason, freed to dream.

In the night, the stars align,
Guiding paths through realms divine.
A tapestry where thoughts can play,
Creating magic, come what may.

Open gates to hidden lands,
Where reality shifts, time expands.
Through portals wide, let visions flow,
In the heart, let visions grow.

The Unseen Tapestry

Threads of fate, woven in time,
Picture stories, lush and prime.
Interlaced with joy and strife,
Crafting all the hues of life.

Colors blend, both bright and dim,
Upon this loom, the world does skim.
Unseen hands with gentle care,
Stitch the moments we all share.

Fingers dance on edges fine,
Patterns shift, and hope does shine.
In each knot, a tale confined,
Every link, a life entwined.

Pull the threads, unravel dreams,
In the weft, the memories gleam.
A masterpiece, both loud and mute,
The stories live, the truth acute.

Underneath the Stars

In the night, where shadows play,
Whispers drift on Milky Way.
Beneath the vast and twinkling dome,
Our thoughts take flight, far from home.

Every star, a distant spark,
Guiding dreams in silver dark.
While constellations softly hum,
A cosmic rhythm, we become.

Lying still on dewy grass,
Counting wishes as they pass.
With each flicker, hearts align,
Beneath the stars, our souls entwine.

In that space, where silence reigns,
The universe reveals its bones.
Underneath the stars so bright,
We stitch our dreams into the night.

Lurking Beneath the Stillness

In silence deep, the shadows creep,
Where secrets hide and silence weeps.
The moonlight casts a silver sheen,
On whispers lost, yet softly seen.

Beneath the calm, a tempest brews,
A world unseen, an ancient muse.
The stillness holds a breath of time,
Where echoes dance in whispered rhyme.

Through quiet paths and hidden trails,
A haunting song, a ghostly wail.
Each rustling leaf, a tale to share,
Of things unseen in cooler air.

When darkness falls, the truth unfolds,
In silent night, the story molds.
Lurking deep, the shadows play,
In every dusk, where dreams hold sway.

Whimsy of the Enigmatic

In twilight's glow, the riddle sways,
As time dissolves in playful lays.
A laugh that dances on the breeze,
With colors bright that tease and please.

The stars above, a fickle game,
Each twinkle holds a different name.
In realms where nothing is as seems,
We wander lost in waking dreams.

The shadows stretch with graceful flair,
A waltz of light through the cool air.
The mystery wraps us in its fold,
With stories untold, in whispers bold.

Embrace the charm of the unknown,
Where whimsies flourish, seeds are sown.
In every turn, a chance to see,
The magic lurking, wild and free.

Veil of Shadows

Beneath the veil where whispers dwell,
A tale unfolds, a silent spell.
The night draws close, as shadows blend,
With secrets waiting, round the bend.

An echo lingers in the dark,
Where dreams ignite a tiny spark.
Lost in the shroud of midnight's hush,
A heartbeat's pulse, a fleeting rush.

The stars, they glimmer, just out of reach,
While silence weaves its gentle preach.
Each moment drips like candle's flame,
In haunting glow, we speak a name.

With every breath, the shadows sway,
In corridors where lost souls play.
Behind the veil, the truth is cast,
A fleeting glimpse of shadows past.

Whispering Dimensions

In layers thick like morning fog,
Where sound dissolves, a quiet smog.
Dimensions curl in stillness tight,
A world beyond the frame of light.

The echoes blend with time and space,
In whispered tones, we find our place.
With every thought, a doorway cracks,
To realms unheard, where fear relax.

Each breath, a thread that weaves the night,
In gentle dreams that take to flight.
With every heartbeat, shapes align,
In the vast web of the divine.

Through whispers soft, connections rise,
In flickers of the unseen skies.
As night retreats from dawn's embrace,
We wander forth in time and space.

Resonance of the Forgotten

In shadows deep where echoes play,
The whispers of the past will sway.
Forgotten tales in silence blend,
A timeless song that will not end.

Memories dance on the edge of night,
Flickering stars, a lost delight.
Voices of those who once were here,
Their laughter lingers, crystal clear.

Tracing steps on old, worn paths,
Unsaid words in fleeting laughs.
The heartbeat of a world once known,
Resonates in whispers, overgrown.

Embrace the silence, yet hold it close,
For in this void, the heart will dose.
The resonance of love, so true,
Binds the forgotten, me and you.

Untold Adventures

In twilight glow, our spirits soar,
Beyond the hills, to distant shore.
With each step taken, dreams unfold,
The path unwinds with tales untold.

Through ancient woods and rivers wide,
Secrets hide where shadows bide.
The call of wild, a siren's song,
To chase the echoes where we belong.

With every heartbeat, new horizons rise,
The world awakens under painted skies.
In quest of wonders, we seek the rare,
Untold adventures await us there.

So raise your sail, let spirits guide,
In the arms of fate, we'll freely ride.
The journey calls, embrace the thrill,
For life's a book, and we write it still.

The Arcane Marketplace

In the heart of night, the lanterns glow,
Stalls of mystery in a lively flow.
Magic whispers, secrets untold,
In the arcane marketplace, brave and bold.

Potions brews in colors bright,
Charmed trinkets glimmering in the light.
Faces masked, with stories to share,
Wanderers seeking treasures rare.

Beneath the stars, the deals are struck,
Enchantments weave with a twist of luck.
In every corner, marvels entwine,
In this hidden realm, fate will align.

As dawn approaches, the magic fades,
Yet in our hearts, its warmth pervades.
A marketplace of dreams held tight,
Where the arcane dances with pure delight.

Unraveled Whispers

In the quiet night, truth takes flight,
As whispers float, dissolving in light.
Fragments of thoughts, lost in the breeze,
Unraveled mysteries, hearts at ease.

The moonlight cradles secrets deep,
Within its glow, the shadows seep.
Words unspoken, dancing on air,
A gentle touch, a silent prayer.

Through tangled paths, we wander far,
Guided softly by a distant star.
The hush of night, a soothing balm,
In whispers soft, the world feels calm.

As dawn approaches, shadows retreat,
Yet echoes linger in the heartbeat.
Unraveled whispers tell our fate,
In every sigh, we celebrate.

Reflections in the Mist

Soft whispers ride the dawn's embrace,
Veils of grey that hide the space.
Mirrored thoughts in hazy glow,
Concealed secrets, slow to show.

Gentle echoes from the deep,
Where memories and dreams still leap.
Mystic forms in silence sway,
In the morning's tender play.

Nature's brush, so lightly pressed,
Tells a story, still unguessed.
With every step, the world transforms,
In these fragments, life warms.

Eyes that search the soft, pale veil,
Finds a truth in every tale.
Within the mist, we lose and find,
A thread of wisdom, deeply entwined.

Shrouded Adventures

Beneath the cloak of twilight's charm,
Bold paths await with open arms.
Whispers call from forest's depth,
In shadows where the heart is kept.

Footsteps trace the hidden ways,
Through the night, where starlight plays.
Every rustle, every sigh,
Speaks of journeys drawing nigh.

Lost in dreams where echoes blend,
Chasing wonders that transcend.
Each moment breathes a new delight,
In the dance of shadows' flight.

Veiled horizons call my name,
In this wild and untamed game.
Adventures wake with dawn's ascent,
With every heartbeat, time is spent.

Nature's Cloaked Wonders

In the folds of the verdant hills,
Nature whispers, softly thrills.
Draped in hues of greenish gold,
Stories waiting to be told.

Underneath the ancient trees,
Secrets stir with every breeze.
Hidden realms of silent grace,
Where time slows down, finds its pace.

Crimson petals, soft and mild,
In the woods, the heart is wild.
Scents of earth and dew embrace,
Miracles in every place.

Marvels wrapped in quiet night,
In the shadows, pure delight.
Nature's beauty, shy and grand,
Invites us to understand.

The Language of Shadows

In the twilight's gentle fold,
Silent stories yearning to be told.
Shadows dance with fleeting grace,
Whispered secrets in their space.

Each silhouette a tale profound,
In the hush, the world unbound.
With every flicker, every glide,
Mysterious truths collide.

Moonlit paths where echoes play,
Guide the soul along its way.
Signs are drawn in muted light,
In the depths of the quiet night.

Listen close; the shadows speak,
In their language, soft and meek.
In their forms, the heart can see,
The art of life's sublimity.

Portals to Another Realm

Through the mist, a doorway glows,
Whispers beckon, the magic flows.
Step inside, where dreams collide,
In shadowed halls, where tales abide.

Stars align in cosmic rhyme,
Time stands still in the sublime.
Lost in echoes, souls entwined,
Unlock the secrets, leave behind.

With every heartbeat, worlds expand,
A flicker sparks, a guiding hand.
Embrace the wonder, chase the light,
In the realm where day meets night.

Portals wait, so vivid, surreal,
Adventures call, it's time to feel.
Beyond the veil, take flight anew,
In the magic, find your view.

Murmurs of Forgotten Places

In the silence where shadows creep,
Ancient ruins softly weep.
Echoes linger of lives once lived,
Whispers of stories, long forgived.

Timeworn paths where memories tread,
Landscapes woven with threads of dread.
Secrets buried, dreams long past,
In the stillness, echoes cast.

Sunlight dances on crumbling stone,
In lonely gardens, seeds are sown.
Murmuring winds through tangled trees,
Revive the tales in fleeting breeze.

Forgotten places call to us,
In hushed tones, they instill trust.
Listen closely, let your heart race,
Unveil the magic of this space.

The Quiet Chronicles

In every breath, a story lies,
A whispered tale beneath the skies.
Soft words penned in twilight's glow,
Chronicled moments that ebb and flow.

Gentle sighs of the moonlit night,
Guide us softly with their light.
Each silence carved, a page unturned,
In stillness, ancient lessons learned.

Books of time in shadows dwell,
Echoes of lives they dare not tell.
But within our hearts, we hold the key,
To read the truths, to set them free.

The quiet whispers of forgotten dreams,
Flow like water in silver streams.
Open your eyes; let the stories bloom,
In this sacred, hallowed room.

Silhouettes of Revelation

Beneath the twilight, shadows grow,
Figures dance in a cosmic flow.
Hidden truths in dark embrace,
Silhouettes whisper in quiet grace.

Shapes emerge from the fading light,
Guiding us through the drawn-out night.
Every outline a secret shared,
In reverie, souls are bared.

Revelations woven in starlit sky,
Dreams unfold as we learn to fly.
In the depths of our silent fears,
We find our courage, wipe our tears.

Silhouettes beckon with a gentle sway,
Leading us to a brand new day.
In this moment, let hearts align,
And embrace the shadows that brightly shine.

Beyond the Veil

Whispers call from shadows deep,
Where ancient secrets seem to sleep.
A flicker of light, a breath of air,
What lies beyond, none can declare.

The moonlight dances on the ground,
In silence, lost, the heart is found.
Threads of fate weave in the night,
Pulling souls towards the light.

Echoes linger, soft and low,
A path unseen, the heart must go.
With every step, the world may shift,
Beyond the veil, the spirits lift.

Through mist and dream, the truth will flow,
In hidden realms, we learn to grow.
The veil may lift to show the way,
Beyond the shadows, we find our stay.

Mysterious Beckoning

A voice calls softly from the woods,
In lullabies of ancient broods.
With tempting whispers on the breeze,
It stirs the heart, entices ease.

Each rustle sings of hidden dreams,
Of paths unseen and silver beams.
A flickering light, a shadow's sway,
Inviting souls to drift away.

The forest holds a magic old,
In every branch, a story told.
A beckoning call, a siren's song,
To follow where the spirits throng.

Through twilight's gate, we slowly tread,
Towards the call, where wonders spread.
What lies ahead, we cannot know,
Yet in the dark, our hearts will glow.

Secrets Amongst the Leaves

In the forest, whispers dwell,
Amongst the leaves, they weave their spell.
Hidden words, like secrets shared,
In every rustling branch, they're bared.

Soft sunlight filters through the green,
Illuminating all that's seen.
The stories held in age-old bark,
Echo softly in the dark.

A dance of shadows, light made real,
Every breeze a gentle feel.
Amongst the leaves, our spirits rise,
Unraveling truth beneath the skies.

Nature's song, so rich and deep,
Calls to those who choose to keep.
The secrets whispered on the breeze,
In every heart, a longing frees.

Woven Wonders

Threads of fate weave life's design,
In colors bright, like stars that shine.
Each moment stitched with care and grace,
Creating dreams in time and space.

From golden dawn to twilight's close,
A tapestry of highs and lows.
Every joy, a vibrant hue,
Every sorrow, deeper too.

Through tangled knots and frayed edges,
We learn to dance on life's ledges.
Each woven wonder tells a tale,
Of love and loss that will not pale.

In every pattern, life unfolds,
A story written, brave and bold.
Woven wonders weave us tight,
In the fabric of the night.

Milton Keynes UK
Ingram Content Group UK Ltd.
UKHW020105041224
451896UK00006B/66